HOLY COWS

HOLY COWS

BY
ILAMAE VINJE WARNES LUND

ILLUSTRATED BY
HARALD AKSDAL

Holy Cows

ISBN: 978-1-935922-71-1

Printed by in the United States of America by
Queen City Printers Inc., Burlington, Vermont

HOLY COWS
is a tribute to my mother.
Her unwavering performance
of the never-ending chores
on our family farm taught me
the ethic of hard work.

Her impeccable
honesty and generosity
in the most austere circumstances
spun the threads that
wove the fabric of my life.

Hold fast to treasured memories
that preserve our past
in warm life-giving color,
dry our tears over life's inevitable losses,
and archive in enviable eternal youth
those whom we have loved.

ILAMAE VINJE WARNES LUND

A THOUSAND THANKS

Of the many challenges a writer faces, the most daunting is expressing adequate gratitude for the team effort that makes even a small book possible.

First, with the longest term of service, is my daughter Kate whose electronic expertise unsnarled the countless computer tangles to which I have been prone through my years of writing, and whose graphic artistry gave credible form to this Christmas story.

My discovery of the inspiring work of Vermont artist Harald Aksdal on the walls of the Enosburg Falls Gallery led to the charming illustrations that give life to my words and carefully capture the scenes in which my Christmas memories were born.

My patient, punctual editor Linda Bland, whose 20-20 vision caught anything and everything that escaped my myopia. Her wisdom led me toward knowing when a story is told and prevented this tale from being twice as long. She is the treasure I found in the shadow of Vermont's Mount Mansfield.

A thousand thank-yous would fall far short of expressing my gratitude to this wonderful team.

From my earliest memory I never took Santa Claus seriously. No one in our family did. Grown-ups spoke of him jokingly, with smiles and a sly wink. Whether he was real or imagined made no difference to me. The fact that Santa never paid us a call had nothing to do with whether I'd been good or bad, nor our isolated location either. Even if he did make regular annual rounds everywhere else, I did not take it as a personal affront that he skipped our house. Any child with eyes could easily see that the rotund Santa could never descend the round black stovepipe ending in the flames of our living room heater.

    I paid much more respect to the Christmas nisse—the tiny red-capped elf—who lived all year long in our attic, observing my good or bad behavior. Now, he was an entity to be reckoned with; at my older sister's encouragement, I dutifully left a small bit of cold leftover mush for him each Christmas Eve to win his favor—just in case.

Holiday rituals were a luxury denied most Iowa farm families who eked out a meager living from the soil in the 1930s. Birthdays and other anniversaries were mostly at-home observances. A favorite meal and a modest homemade gift were considered adequate celebration for our family of seven. Of course, there were happy memorable moments, but they were always brief, sandwiched into cracks of time stolen from ongoing tasks; any job left undone could threaten the survival of our farming family. This stark ever-present necessity placed rituals at the bottom of the list, far below chores.

The word chores was a wastebasket holding everything: One long list of divergent tasks requiring daily completion before any optional activities could be considered. Chores meant anything "too important to put off." And there were many. Chores were what farming was all about—not rituals or leisure.

The first Christmas tree I remember stood in our parlor when I was four; it was the first tree after the death of my father two years before. This loss had plunged our home into extended grief and diminished hope; holidays and birthdays were now barely noted. But if any celebration could rise from the ashes of such sadness that holiday was Christmas.

I sensed I was the main reason for the extra effort that year: so the youngest in the family could marvel at the splendor of a candle-lit tree. This meant the added chore of tree cutting for someone, in this case my brother. He hiked to Uncle Nels' grove on the far corner of our farm and pulled a five-foot fir home on my sled.

Each candle was inserted into a substantial tin base that in turn clipped onto a carefully selected branch that held it upright at a safe distance from branches above. My mother prepared a pail of water to stand at-the-ready should an errant candle ignite neighboring fir needles. Simple, mostly homemade gifts, and not many, were placed under the tree. If there were any gifts from a store, they never exceeded 50 cents in price. One present costing a dollar was considered extravagant, unthinkable.

That same Christmas Eve, when supper dishes had been washed and put away, my two older sisters and I were cozily seated around the tree glowing with candles. Mother presided nearby with the pail full of water. Into this peaceful stillness, a loud thumping and clattering erupted on the porch. Everyone's mouth dropped open.

Nobody ever arrived in winter's darkness up our lane, now obscured by snowdrifts—most certainly not on Christmas Eve. Wild-eyed and fearful, I ran to Mother's side, hiding my eyes in the folds of her apron until giggles of my sisters encouraged me to look up.

A tall figure in a cap with fur-lined earflaps and a muffler covering his face, lumbered into the room. He was lugging a large package loosely covered with brown paper. I was the last to recognize my brother, the eldest in our family and surrogate father to me for the rest of my life.

He carefully placed the large package next to our mother's chair. The gift was a complete surprise to us all: a splendid shining white and green kitchen stool for our work-worn mother's comfort and convenience.

My big brother's selfless gift, purchased after weeks of sequestering a few cents at a time, gave us as much joy as if we had given the gift ourselves. His unexpected and dramatic entrance came closest to a visit from Santa that I can remember.

The next Christmas Eve stands out in my childhood, more memorable than the kitchen stool.

The time for evening chores was the dread of my life during winter. I was terrified, left alone in our dark house, lit only by a kerosene lamp; its feeble radiance did not reach even the corners of the kitchen—let alone the soot-black darkness of the rest of our house.

When everyone went to the barn for evening milking, feeding, and bedding, I was left inside to panic. From the moment I watched their bundled-up shadows leaving with their lantern light, I sat waiting by the kitchen window, eyes fixed on the small barn window through which a dim ray soon glowed.

I prayed for the moment that lantern light would leave the window, emerge through the barn door, and the dark figures of my family would trudge back to the house. Meanwhile, I sat trembling, sending occasional glances at the blackness behind the huge kitchen woodstove. I was certain a legion of monsters lived there, ready to pounce on me if I stirred.

I had often pleaded to be taken along to the barn; but the troublesome extra effort of bundling up a child, who could only stand leaning against the wall while others performed evening chores, did not seem to Mother worth the trouble.

One exception was this unforgettable Christmas Eve: When my mother began dressing me for the cold walk to the barn, I was thrilled. I stealthily kept my wondering to myself, though I was overjoyed at this surprise. I trudged along as quickly as I could behind my mother and older sister, for the long trek through snow that sometimes reached near my waist.

Once inside I was placed safely behind
the row of cows, as Mother milked one after
another. Little drew my attention except the
puffs of vapor rising from the cows' noses and
an occasional whisk of a tail. Little could be
heard except the rhythmic metallic tings of
milk against the side of the pail. I did not
mind the long wait, for I was spared the terror
of waiting in the dark kitchen.

By the time my mother had milked the last
of our ten cows, my sister would be almost
finished with the cream separating task in
the milk house. Usually this signaled a hurried
trip back to the house and the warmth of
our kitchen.

On this particular evening, this Christmas Eve, Mother seemed less hurried. She bedded down each cow in her stanchion, giving more fresh straw than usual and an extra handful of alfalfa hay in each feedbox. As Mother did this, she murmured soothingly to each animal, using the cow's name: Plum, Daisy, Blossom, Elmira… I watched as she tenderly stroked each animal's neck.

This was unusual behavior, even for my gentle mother who, judging by her frequent complaints, detested the twice-a-day milking chore. She continued similar motherly attention to the calves in nearby pens.

Miles from the nearest church, this holiest of nights was observed through my mother's faithful attendance to routine tasks. By the dim light of a lantern, our barn became her manger. Without benefit of clergy, without choral anthems or scripture texts, my mother's observance was her quiet gestures of kindness and comfort to the animals who constituted our family's livelihood—our life.

For a few brief moments, a peace on earth—a holiness—infused the contented stillness. Even in my child's mind, I perceived the connection. Wordlessly I watched her perform this liturgy. It marked this night as different from the rest.

It seemed too soon to leave this hallowed stillness and plod our return to the house and warmth. Empty milk pails rattled at the ends of my arms; the cream can and unwieldy separator parts were carried by others.

Once inside, we unwrapped ourselves from our cold heavy garments and lifted them to their nails beside the door.

We embraced the warmth around the huge Monarch range; the pitch darkness behind it had now lost its sinister threat. Our warm supper would soon be ladled out.

After that, even more household chores awaited, before time for slumber in the unheated bedrooms upstairs; the wisps of our own exhaled breaths would rise above our noses until Christmas morning.

This was a Christmas Eve I have remembered for a lifetime. By the flickering lantern in our barn I had learned of the sanctity of work. Chores to me had always been the bad word that limited fun; chores shortened my sister's free time to play with me. And chores restricted our time at the county fair for one last 10-cent carousel ride.

Without a word, my mother had taught me a lesson, through quiet conscientious performance of her never-ending chores: Ritual can be a sincere observance of the heart, without a sanctified place of worship and the accoutrements of candlelight and choral music.

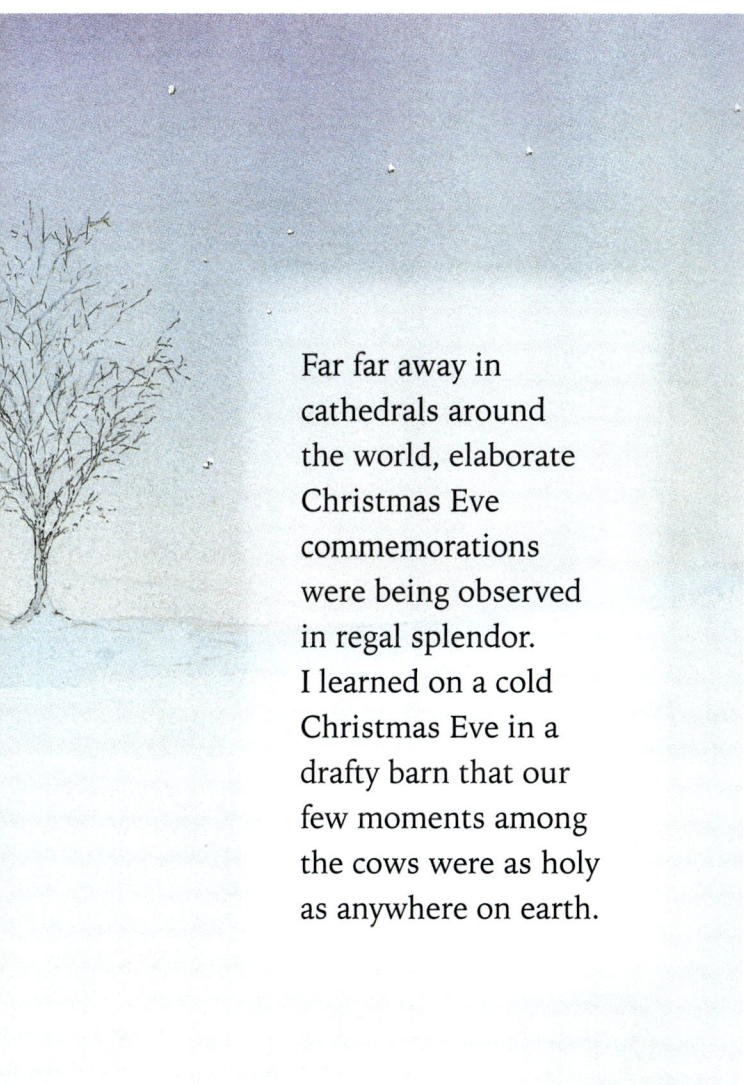

Far far away in
cathedrals around
the world, elaborate
Christmas Eve
commemorations
were being observed
in regal splendor.
I learned on a cold
Christmas Eve in a
drafty barn that our
few moments among
the cows were as holy
as anywhere on earth.

ABOUT THE AUTHOR

Ilamae Vinje Warnes Lund is the fifth and youngest of the Vinje family, born on their small farm in Worth County, Iowa. Her education began in a one-room schoolhouse; she graduated from St. Olaf College then taught high school in Montana and Oregon. Lund's first book, *Why Gramma Kept Herself in Stitches* focuses on the benefits of hand arts during periods of stress. She anticipates completing a collection of memoir short stories entitled *The Spoon Holder* in 2015. Lund resides in a cottage on the shore of St. Albans Bay in Vermont near her daughter. Her son Lloyd lives in Oregon. She posts her news, stories, and occasional poetry on her blog: ILAMAELUND.WORDPRESS.COM.

ABOUT THE ILLUSTRATOR

Vermont artist Harald Aksdal lives with his wife Becky
in the foothills of the Green Mountains in Vermont. His
artistic talent transferred easily from architect to artist
as a second career painting with watercolors. Aksdal
exhibits throughout New England and in a cooperative
gallery in Enosburg Falls, Vermont.
His work can be found
at AKSDALART.COM.